A Needleworker's Botany

111988

FIFTY EXAMPLES OF EARLY BOTANICAL
ART FROM THE LIBRARY OF THE
MASSACHUSETTS HORTICULTURAL
SOCIETY ADAPTED FOR NEEDLEWORK

Heather S. Miller

NEW HAMPSHIRE
PUBLISHING COMPANY
SOMERSWORTH

Library of Congress Catalog Card Number 78-59803
ISBN (hardbound) 0-912274-81-6
ISBN (softbound) 0-912274-99-9
Copyright © by Heather S. Miller
Printed in the United States of America
Design by Wladislaw Finne

Contents

Preface

Much interesting information and many beautiful works of art are preserved in the libraries of the world. Unfortunately, even when these libraries are open to the public, the books on their shelves, especially older ones, are generally much less accessible than the treasures of a museum, partly because relatively few people know where to look for the kind of art-work found in books.

This book is an attempt to bring to public view some examples of early botanical art, only one kind of art found between the covers of books, and to show that these drawings are not merely curiosities but are part of the history of our culture, are interesting and beautiful to look at, and can be put to practical use today as designs for needleworkers. No doubt artists and craftsmen working in other media will find them useful, too. It is also my hope that the historical and botanical information accompanying the illustrations will appeal to persons interested in plants and art as well as in needlework.

The unique resources of the Massachusetts Horticultural Society Library have made this book possible. I have chosen to present only one aspect of this rich and extensive collection here and that for a purpose never imagined by its founders. I am indebted to those who originally developed this remarkable library in 1829 and to those who have maintained it since its beginning.

Grateful acknowledgment is made of the information and inspiration obtained from the works listed in the bibliography of basic needlework books, which follows the illustrations. Creative needleworkers have been an inspiration wherever their work has been encountered. I would also like to express my appreciation to the Bentham-Moxon Trust, current publishers of *Curtis's Botanical Magazine*.

Special thanks go to family and friends for their enthusiasm and encouragement and especially to Norton Miller for advice and assistance.

Introduction

PLANTS IN OUR LIVES

Today, in an increasingly impersonal and mechanized world, we establish a line of communication with nature when we raise plants in and around our homes. Similarly, handwork brings to our lives a personal touch, a link with primitive cultures, former times, and the earth itself as we put natural fibers to use and employ motifs taken from nature in our designs. And we can combine the two, plant motifs and handwork, to further increase our link with the natural world.

As long as man has existed, plants have been part of his life, first as a source of food and fuel and later as a source of medicine, dyes, fibers, and myriad commercial products. At first wild plants were simply gathered for food. Prehistoric man seems not to have used plant images as he used the images of animals in his art. Perhaps the uncertainty and danger of the hunt required magical images to ensure good fortune while the stationary plants were more dependable sources of food. Early Stone Age plant forms scratched on bone have been found, but plant motifs did not become important in art until the development of agriculture in the Neolithic age (roughly 7000 B.C. in the Middle East and Asia). With the much later use of plants for their medicinal properties, the picturing of plants became more frequent.

The earliest known botanical book was found at the Great Temple of Thutmose III at Karnak in Egypt where 275 plants are pictured in limestone relief. Among these plants are some familiar to us now, such as the pomegranate. These reliefs date from the fifteenth century B.C. Stone reliefs of lilies dating from the early seventh century B.C. have been found near Nineveh. The great civilizations of Assyria, Crete, Greece, and Rome all utilized plant designs, often highly decorative, on jars, murals, coins, cups, and other objects. Throughout the Christian era plants have been a popular element in western art of all kinds from works by the great painters to folk art, tapestries, quilts, samplers, rugs, jewelry, and metalwork. If possible, visit an art or natural history museum and look for plant motifs. You'll find them on objects and works of art from all cultures and ages. The beauty, symmetry, and delicacy of plant life have universal appeal.

PLANTS IN BOOKS

With the exception of Laurence's book on gardening, all the books represented here attempted to present to their readers scientific descriptions of plants, many of which had never before been seen by Europeans. The intellectual origins of these books go beyond antiquity, to the desire to know and understand the world around us. The earlier books represented here trace their origins directly back to Dioscorides's *De Materia Medica*, an encyclopedia of medicinal plants written in the first century A.D.

By the early eighteenth century much knowledge about the natural world had accumulated. Outlooks and understanding were being expanded steadily through travel, exploration, new discoveries, better communication, and other advances. This gradual expansion of knowledge, of tolerance for new ideas, and the ever-growing quest for the undiscovered was a legacy of the Renaissance. During the eighteenth century this heritage gave birth to the Enlightenment, with its belief in human reason, natural order, and progress, and it was this age that produced Carl Linnaeus, a man who gave the science of botany a push forward so strong that its effects are still felt.

Prior to the eighteenth century plants had names, of course, but many methods of naming were used, and names were long and elaborate. Almost every botanist had his own name for every plant. Carl Linnaeus applied his organizational ability to this chaotic situation and created a simple, orderly method of classifying, naming, and describing all plants, animals and minerals. His first books were published in 1735; he eventually published a total of eighty-seven.

Linnaeus was a genius, a man with tremendous energy, a faultless memory, and a well-developed ego. He accomplished single-handedly what was no less than a revolution in botanical circles. His methods were influential throughout the eigteenth and nineteenth centuries and into the twentieth. Linnaeus's system of naming plants is the basis for modern scientific plant nomenclature.

Briefly, the method described by Linnaeus in 1735 in his book *Systema Naturae* provided for arranging all plants in twenty-four groups based on the number and condition of the stamens (pollen-producing floral parts). In place of long descriptive phrases, plant names were reduced to two Latin words, so that each plant received a unique name indicative of its place in the classification system and generally descriptive of its characteristics. The clarity and simplicity of this system gained many adherents, especially since more and more plants were being discovered each year. Linnaeus gathered around himself a group of dedicated disciples and students who traveled the world collecting plants for his work. There were also disciples he never met who adopted his system for their own use and in turn taught it to their students. Some of the books represented here were the result of work by these followers.

The new system went hand in hand with accelerating exploration and discovery during the eighteenth century. Both the eighteenth and nineteenth centuries have been called The Golden Age of Plant Hunting, the culmination of steadily increasing activity during the preceding centuries. During this period many dedicated and courageous people suffered great hardships and sometimes gave their lives while exploring and studying remote parts of the world. Numerous new plants were introduced to western science in this way, including many now familiar cultivated plants. In order to spread the word about these exciting new discoveries, descriptions and illustrations of them were published in books or magazines. Fifty of these illustrations are reproduced in this book.

BOTANICAL ILLUSTRATION

Botanical illustration is a very special joining of plants and art. The uses of plants in art that have been mentioned so far have adopted plant motifs for the sake of art. Botanical illustration puts art to work for the sake of plants. It is the depiction of plants for instruction so that these plants are recognizable to the viewer. Therefore the plant cannot be stylized and must be presented as nearly as possible as it appears in nature. It is sometimes said that illustration is not art, but art, design, and science are all evident in the illustrations reproduced here.

It is thought that many botanical books of antiquity were accompanied by illustrations, now lost, which were copied many times and appear in adulterated form in early books of the Christian era. Several early manuscripts of Dioscorides's *De Materia Medica* contain fine botanical illustrations. Until the early fifteenth century formal botanical art remained unoriginal and even largely inaccurate, but with the dawning of the Renaissance botanical art was again infused with spirit and originality.

When printing was developed during the fifteenth century the way was prepared for the reproduction of illustrations along with printed texts. Several methods of reproducing illustrations were eventually developed.

The earliest were the woodcut, in which the design was cut into the side of a board, and the wood engraving, in which the end grain of a block of wood was used. The use of metal plates for printing had been known for some time before it was employed in botanical illustration at the end of the sixteenth century. A line engraving is made by pushing a tool called a burin over a copper plate, cutting the design into the plate. To make an etching, acid is used to cut the design into the metal.

In the printing process woodcuts or wood engravings take the ink on their raised portions, but metal plates take the ink in the grooves cut into the plates by the burin or the acid. When passed through the press the ink resting in the grooves is forced onto the paper. The use of metal plates was a more laborious and expensive process that produced illustrations with finer detail and more precision than the wood block prints. These remained the means of reproducing botanical art in the West until the nineteenth century, when the technique of lithography came into prominence. Most of the illustrations reproduced here were made by the earlier methods utilizing metal plates. All were printed in black and white. If colored illustrations were desired, the printed pictures were painstakingly painted by hand.

The books chosen for inclusion here represent a cross section of European botanical illustration from the sixteenth to nineteenth centuries, but they are not meant to be a capsule history in themselves. They were chosen to represent a broad spectrum in terms of time periods, styles, and plants depicted. The illustrations are arranged chronologically, based on the publication dates of the books they were taken from, except for the pictures from Joseph Banks's *Illustrations of Australian Plants* which was not published until the twentieth century although the drawings were prepared about 1770. Bolton's books are grouped together under the earliest title page date. Choice of illustrations was also based on adaptability for needlework and availability of the books.

The illustrations have not been altered, although separate elements that appeared

Here is a one-of-a-kind article of clothing, a shirt embroidered by Rosemary Swan of East Lebanon, Maine, based on the tree design from John Laurence's book The Clergyman's Recreation. *Six strand cotton embroidery floss was used on a purchased cotton shirt.*

One of the ferns pictured in Reede's Hortus Indicus Malabaricus was used as a design by John Swan of Rye, New Hampshire. His small latch hook rug was worked in one hundred percent polyester yarn with shades of green on a cream-colored background. The unique quality of the plant has been captured in this piece that seems too beautiful to walk on.

on the original plates, such as roots, labels, and seeds, may have been omitted. The scientific names identifying each plant are those in use today.

USING THE ILLUSTRATIONS

This is not a pattern book. It is intended to be a source book of motifs and ideas. Basic "how-to" instructions for various types of needlework are not included, nor are full instructions or charts given or yarns and colors prescribed. This book is intended not to show you how to create an exact replica of someone else's design, but to enable you to create an original piece of needlework, uniquely your own. Among these illustrations you will find designs suitable for embroidery in all its many variations, including needlepoint, mixed forms combining appliqué, quilting and embroidery, and rug hooking. Some are especially suitable for traditional rug hooking with its possibilities for achieving fine detail and delicate shading. If doing needlepoint you will probaby want to use a small mesh canvas, such as 18 mesh, in order to capture as much fine detail as possible. The things you can use these designs for are limitless: clothing, linens, utilitarian objects, wall hangings and pictures, rugs, bags, and so on.

If you are a novice and need basic instruction, don't be discouraged. Needlework classes are offered by individuals, shops, and adult education programs. In addition, many books that enable you to teach yourself are available at public libraries or local bookstores. Some of these are listed at the end of this book.

No matter how inexperienced or advanced a needleworker you are, there are designs here for you. Don't be afraid of them: adapt, simplify, embellish, use them in ways not mentioned here. Borders can be added, and designs or parts of designs can be repeated to form borders themselves. Designs can be repeated to form larger motifs. The discoverers of these plants were not bound by tradition; don't let these illustrations bind you to their form. Use them to discover new plant forms and new ways of using them. Have courage; don't let rules destroy your enthusiasm.

Once you decide on a design and how you want to use it, you need to transfer it from the book to your fabric. First trace the design onto tracing paper. Then if you want the design larger or smaller than the size given here, place your tracing on top of a sheet of graph paper. The vertical and horizontal lines will show through and thus can easily be transferred to the tracing. Mark off the even squares, using a ruler for accuracy. In order to enlarge a design, you must redraw it onto paper marked with larger squares; to reduce it, you need to copy it into smaller squares. Graph paper is obtainable in large sheets with squares of various sizes, and using it is much easier than attempting to draw your own lines on plain paper, although this can be done. If your tracing is marked in ¼-inch squares and you want to double it, copy it into ½-inch squares. To reduce it by half, mark your tracing in ½-inch squares and copy it into ¼-inch squares. Similar adjustments permit enlarging or reducing any design by any other amount. It is helpful to number the squares along the top and left side on both the tracing and the graph paper for easy reference. Now, beginning at the upper left corner, begin copying the design square by square, reproducing exactly the part of the design in square number one on your tracing in square number one of the graph paper. The only difference should be in the size of the two drawings. The following diagram shows how this is done. In this case the mushrooms are doubled in size.

Several mechanical aids for enlarging and reducing designs are available in needlework shops. It is also possible to have the picture photostatted to the correct size. This method costs several dollars but is quick and easy. On the other hand some people like to go through the process of enlarging or reducing the design by hand because it gives them more of a feel for the design before they begin the actual stitchery.

Once you have the design drawn to the desired size you are ready to transfer it to the fabric. Designs may be transferred to sheer fabrics by tracing from the drawing with water color paints. They can be traced onto rug or tapestry canvas using special felt tip markers made for this purpose. If you want to know exactly where each color should go, paint in the design with acrylics. Dressmaker's carbon paper, available in light or dark colors, can be used to transfer designs to smooth fabrics. When using this carbon paper, place the fabric on a smooth, hard surface with the carbon paper on top, coated side down. Place the design on the carbon paper and go over it carefully with a hard pencil. There is also available an iron-on design transfer pencil suitable for many fabrics that can take a hot iron. With this method, once your design is drawn on tracing paper, you go over the

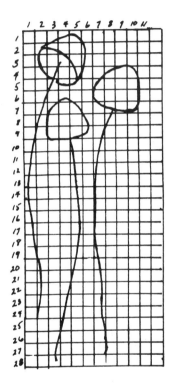

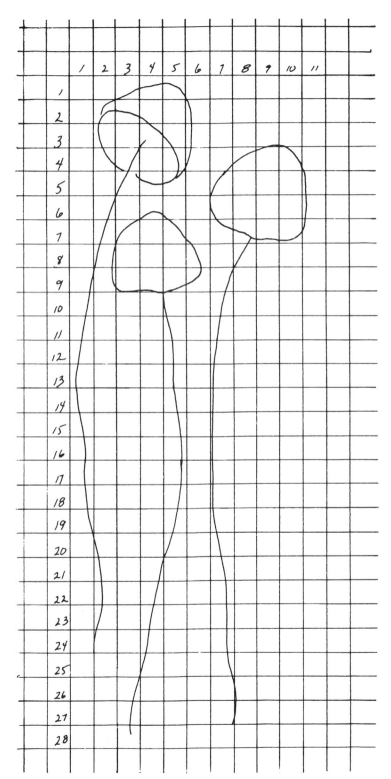

For a touch of spring in December, three Christmas tree ornaments were made from designs in Duhamel's Traité des arbres fruitiers, *Banks's* Illustrations of Australian Plants *and Curtis's* Botanical Magazine. *Rayon embroidery thread was used on satin fabric. Each ornament was stuffed with polyester fiberfill to give it a three-dimensional quality, and then finished with corded edging. A crocheted loop was added for hanging. A similar technique could be used to make sachets, pincushions, or pillows. (Made by the author.)*

back of each line with this pencil. The paper is then placed on the fabric and a hot iron is used to transfer the lines to the fabric. In order to transfer a design to a fabric with knap, put the final design on tracing paper and sew it to the fabric with small stitches, stitching along every line of the design, and then carefully tear away the paper.

"Prick and pounce" is a professional and dependable, although time-consuming, method of transferring designs. It involves marking the fabric with dots of chalk forced through holes pricked in the paper on which the design is drawn. To do this, place the design on a soft surface, such as a towel, and with a needle carefully prick holes one sixteenth to one eighth of an inch apart along every line. Use a smaller needle and closer spacing for lighter weight fabric and a larger needle and wider spacing on heavier fabric. Then carefully pin or baste the pricked design onto the fabric. Pounce is powdered chalk or charcoal; talcum powder is an adequate substitute. Roll a cylinder of several thicknesses of felt and overcast the seam. Use the end of the roll to rub pounce over the design, forcing the powder through the holes and thereby leaving dots of powder to show the design on the fabric. Since the powder is very impermanent, the outline of the design is next painted in using a water-based paint and fine brush.

Once the design appears in final form on the fabric with the edges appropriately secured and fastened to a frame, stretcher, or embroidery hoop, you can more clearly envision the final product. You probably have a good idea of colors and stitches you want to use. The real color of flowers in the fifty illustrations in this book has been indicated whenever possible, but feel free to use other colors if you wish. Shading is apparent in many of the pictures. If you want to create a shaded effect where it is not indicated, look at the way light falls on plants around your home, and then improvise.

Look at your design in its ready-to-go state to see if you are still happy with your plan for colors and stitches. If you're unsure of how you want to do part of it, go ahead with other parts. As you work, the solutions to problem parts will suggest themselves. If you want to use unfamiliar stitches, practice them on scrap fabric until you can produce a consistently uniform, smooth stitch. Complicated stitches are unnecessary. Striking results can be obtained with a few simple stitches. Use colors that please you and combine with each other for the effect you want. Always use good quality materials.

The final word on using the illustrations is simply *use* them, in whatever ways you wish. The plant world offers infinite variety, forms, and beauty too remarkable to be imagined by man. These illustrations show this variety and beauty with a clarity and sensitivity that comes only with a deep knowledge and love of the plant world. They were the result of work by adventuresome, creative lovers of the natural world and are offered to needleworkers in the hope that they will be used in the same spirit.

A Selection of Botanical Art

1592
Phytobasanos

The first purely botanical book illustrated with prints made from metal plates was published in 1592. Called *Phytobasanos,* which means "plant touchstone," it was written by Fabio Colonna, a Neapolitan lawyer whose many interests included languages, music, mathematics, and art as well as botany. Colonna suffered from epilepsy, and it is believed that his interest in botany grew out of his search for a cure to his affliction. This search led him to the herb Valerian, which had been prescribed for this condition by the Greek surgeon Dioscorides, in his *De Materia Medica* published in the first century A.D. Whether Colonna found himself cured is disputed, but his interest in botanical studies continued to grow. He described many new plants, clarified obscure passages in Dioscorides, and in general revived Italian interest in the study of botany.

Out of Colonna's knowledge and love of plants developed this small book, for which he produced his own illustrations and etchings. Although he was only twenty-four years old when the book was published—he was born in Naples in 1567—it represented a significant step forward in the study of botany because of the high quality of his scholarship and illustrations. In later years the book was expanded and republished. In these editions, the plants were arranged so that similar ones were grouped together. This was an early, if not the first, attempt at systematically classifying plants, an accomplishment finally achieved by Linnaeus in the early eighteenth century.

The plant depicted here, *Aquilegia vulgaris,* is a delicate perennial herb with white flowers that grows in Europe. As a design it could be used for embroidery, perhaps using silk or rayon thread on white organdy to make a pillow that would give a light, airy touch to a summer porch. The decorative border surrounding the plant, which is an unusual feature in botanical illustration, could be reproduced as is, or it could be the inspiration for another of your own devising.

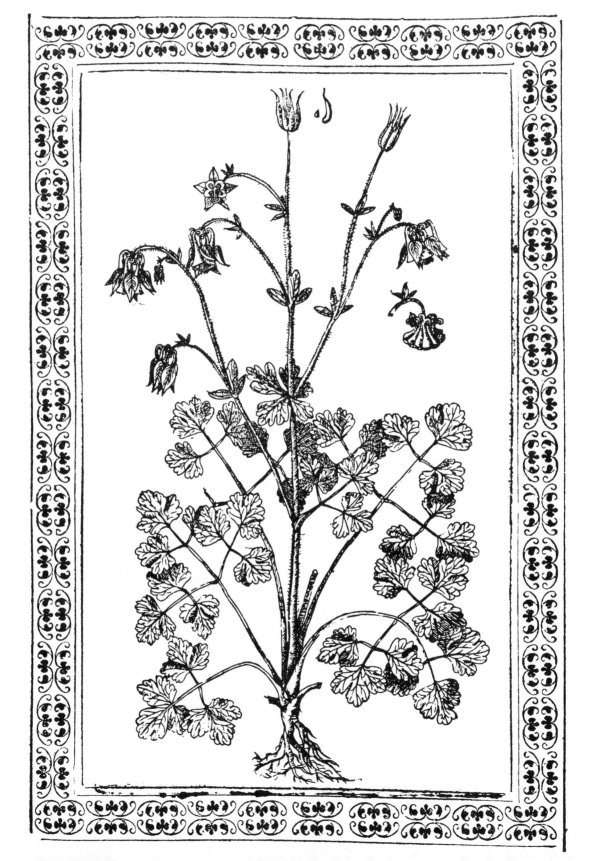

1678
Hortus Indicus Malabaricus

Hendrik Adriaan van Reede tot Drakestein was a Dutch nobleman who served with the East India Company in many capacities, including that of Governor of Malabar, a colony on the southwestern coast of India. A talented amateur naturalist, he expended considerable energy studying the flora of the region he governed. He employed hundreds of Indians to collect plants for him and four native artists to make drawings from the live specimens. Years of such effort resulted in the eventual publication of his twelve-volume work, *Hortus Indicus Malabaricus*, which was one of the earliest European studies of Indian plants and one of the most famous studies of fauna or flora published before the time of Linnaeus.

From the drawings by the native artists, Father Mathieu, a Carmelite from Goa and also an amateur botanist, made the copper engravings from which these plates were made. Some authorities believe that Father Mathieu also worked on some of the drawings, and others think that van Reede himself may have contributed some. In any case, the resulting work contained true-to-size illustrations that are remarkable for their clarity, vitality, and strength. Most plates bear the name of the plant in Latin, Malabaric, Hindi, and Arabic. The twelve volumes in this work were published over a twenty-five year period, between 1678 and 1703, and have caused bibliographers considerable difficulty due to various inconsistencies and errors on the title pages, some of which show the fourth volume to have been published in 1673. The title of the book itself also varies. Van Reede died in 1691, so the last several volumes were released posthumously.

The four plants pictured here, which are all reprinted from volume 12, are robust tropicals suited to being worked in bold materials and bright colors. The first picture shows the fern that was the basis for the latch hook rug shown on page 18. The second is a leaf of *Raphidophora*, a climbing plant of the tropical forests in the same family as the familiar Philodendron. A striking effect could be achieved by using this large single leaf for appliqué. The third plate shows another fern, and the fourth, a sedge. The latter picture indicates more motion than is usual in botanical art and would make a lively embroidered motif.

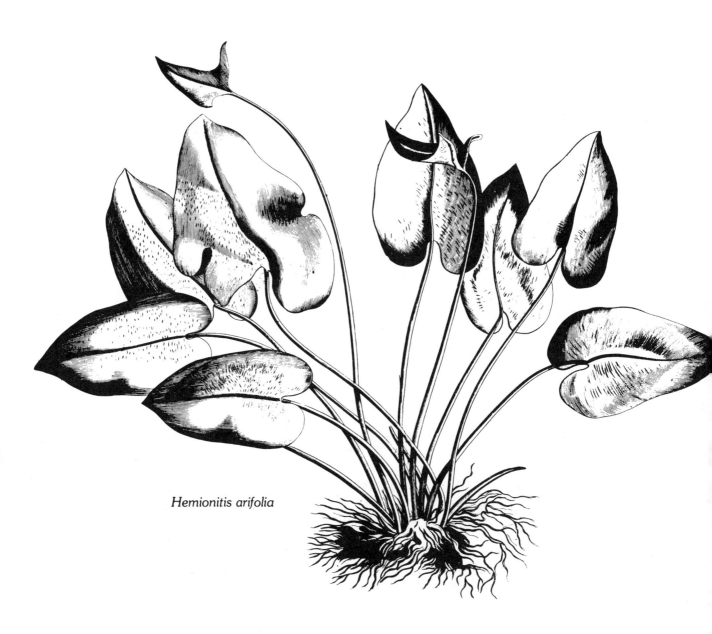

Hemionitis arifolia

Raphidophora pertusa

Adiantum lunulatum

Cyperus kyllingia

33

1717
The Clergyman's Recreation

England has long been the home of many dedicated hobby gardeners. Among them was John Laurence, a clergyman who lived from 1668 to 1732 and pursued experimental gardening in his spare time. He began his hobby with the abandoned garden of his first rectory, in Yelvertoft, Northamptonshire. Boasting clay soil and a mass of weeds surrounded by mud walls when he began, the garden produced at least eight different kinds of fruit after only a few years under his care. Some twenty years of experience went into Laurence's first book, *The Clergyman's Recreation Shewing the Pleasure and Profit of the Art of Gardening*. It was so popular that six editions were issued in the twelve years following its first appearance in 1714.

Much of Laurence's work was innovative, and others often did not believe the results of his experiments. He was a careful and accurate gardener, however, and when other experimenters repeated his efforts they found his conclusions to be correct. Laurence's book is of particular historical interest to horticulturists, because it includes one of the earliest published reports of a virus being transmitted by grafting.

The illustration shown here is from the fifth edition, published in 1717. It was drawn to demonstrate the correct method of growing fruit trees against a wall, the way Laurence grew his own trees in the rectory garden. It appears here in skeletal form to be left plain or to be embellished, as you wish. It could become a striking picture worked in crewel yarn with the addition of leaves in various shades of green, flowers, birds, squirrels, or red-ripe apples along the branches. Or you might try working grass and wildflowers, fallen leaves, or apples underneath. In both cases, no more than a few simple stitches—such as the satin stitch, back stitch, straight stitch, long and short stitch, and French knots—would be needed. Another possibility would be to create a simple and decorative family tree with names inserted on appropriate branches. The tree would also make an interesting series of wall hangings or pillows illustrating the four seasons, with colors and added features representing the essentials of each. This design was used to decorate the back of the shirt shown on page 17.

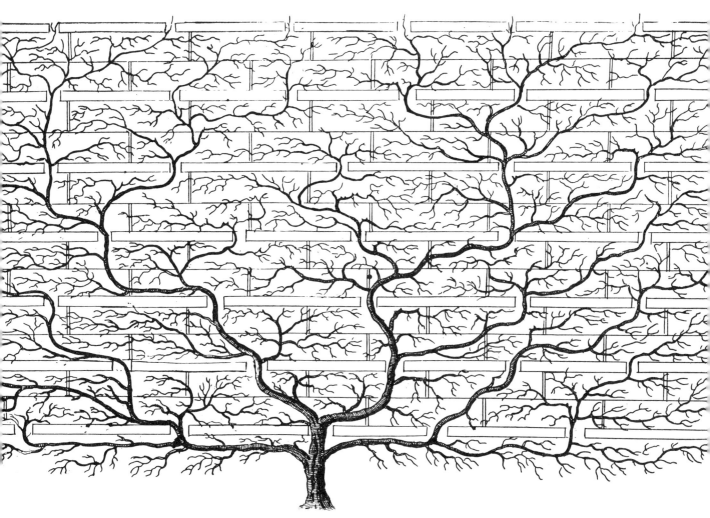

A fruit tree

1741
Herbarium Amboinense

George Everard Rumpf's *Herbarium Amboinense* ranks with van Reede's *Hortus Indicus Malabaricus* as a major early account of flora in the colonial East Indies. The title means "plant collections from Amboyna." Rumpf was a Dutch doctor with the East India Company on the Indonesian island of Amboyna and like van Reede, an energetic naturalist. This work came to fruition only because of his fierce determination: to complete the material he overcame blindness, which struck him at the age of 43, the burning of his papers and specimens, the loss of part of the manuscript, and the death of his wife, his constant companion and assistant.

Actual publication of the *Herbarium Amboinense* was undertaken thirty-nine years after Rumpf's death by Johannes Burman, one of the great promoters of the Linnaean system of classification. The illustrations for the six-volume set were prepared by several artists. Rumpf and his great *Herbarium Amboinense* have been the subject of two noted studies published in the twentieth century: *The Rumphius Memorial Volume* (Amsterdam, 1959) and *An Interpretation of Rumphius' Herbarium Amboinense* (Manila, 1917).

The two tropical plants pictured here are reprinted from the fifth volume. They could be used to make embroidered pictures or pillows and would be attractive done in crewel or other embroidery. The bulbous plant is *Crinum latifolium* var. *zeylanicum*, a relative of the familiar Amaryllis. Its flowers are white marked with purple, a coloring that has given rise to the common name of Milk and Wine Lily. The second plate depicts the bottle gourd *Lagenaria siceraria*, whose pale tan or greenish fruits are used for making dippers, utensils, birdhouses, and other objects.

Crinum latifolium var. zeylanicum

37

Lagenaria siceraria

1768
Traité des Arbres Fruitiers

Henry Louis Duhamel du Monceau, who was born in 1700 to an aristocratic family, is the author of numerous fine botanical works. He studied natural science with single-minded enthusiasm and eventually became a fellow of most of the major European scientific societies of his day. He held the position of Inspector General in France's Departement de la Marine, where he oversaw the construction and condition of ships, sails, and riggings and studied the preservation of the wood used in the ships. His interest in plants with economic value was reinforced by this occupation and by the travel to the world's ports that it permitted him.

Duhamel's work and his botanical pursuits absorbed all his energies; he never married and used all his income for his studies and publications. He was one of those eighteenth century gentlemen who, by the high standards of their work and its constant application to the welfare of humanity, helped make science respectable.

Traité des arbres fruitiers, Duhamel's fine study of fruit trees, was first published in 1768, and it is from that edition that these plants are reproduced. Of the several well-known artists who contributed the drawings for the book's 118 plates, the most outstanding was Claude Aubriet. Although the unassuming Aubriet was not highly educated, he was remarkably skillfull in drawing plants. In the days before photography, such a talent was invaluable to botanists, and Aubriet became a good friend of many noted botanists. His name is commemorated in the lovely garden plant *Aubrieta.* The book itself was for many years *the* book for fruit growers. Its scope was greatly increased in the early nineteenth century by two other outstanding botanical artists, Pierre Antoine Poiteau and Pierre Jean François Turpin, whose additions made it "one of the most splendid books on fruit ever produced."

The three familiar fruits depicted here, cherry, apple, and strawberry, are the works of some of the other artists who contributed to the first edition of *Traité des arbres fruitiers.* They would make an attractive set of embroidered pictures, with all three worked in harmonious but not identical shades of red contrasting with the greens of the leaves and the white flesh of the apple. Part of the strawberry was used in one of the Christmas tree ornaments pictured on page 22.

Prunus avium

40

Malus pumila

Fragaria vesca

42

1770
Illustrations of Australian Plants

The drawings in *Illustrations of Australian Plants* were produced under great hardship and were eagerly awaited by the scientific community in the late 1770s, but it was not until the beginning of the twentieth century that they were finally published. Not even the pleas of Linneaus were successful in making them available.

The material in this long overdue volume was gathered on a trip around the world aboard the *Endeavour* with Captain James Cook. The expedition, which lasted from 1768-1770, was organized by Joseph Banks, a self-taught naturalist whose interest in botany was kindled at the age of fifteen on a beautiful summer day while walking along a flower-lined English country lane. He devoted almost his entire life to botany and had explored England, Newfoundland, Labrador, and Portugal before undertaking his trip around the world.

After visiting Tahiti and New Zealand, the *Endeavour* made the east coast of Australia (then called New Holland) on April 19, 1770; the crew named their landfall Botany Bay. Banks and his assistant, Daniel Solander, explored this coastline until the end of August, collecting and writing copious notes on everything they saw. The two men realized that they had come upon an entirely new flora in a land whose climate and vegetation held great promise for European colonization.

Homeward bound, the ship suffered considerable damage on the Australian reefs, and six of the ten expedition members in Banks's party, including all three artists, died during the voyage. But Banks and Solander returned with huge plant collections, seeds, nearly 1,000 drawings, and volumes of manuscript notes. The trip opened a new era in scientific exploration and added considerably to European knowledge of astronomy, zoology, botany, and anthropology.

Once back in London, the task of organizing and describing the material preparatory to publication fell to Solander. Work proceeded slowly and publication was promised over and over again. When Solander died in 1782 progress halted, for Banks was completely absorbed by his many other activities, among them supervising the Royal Botanic Garden at Kew, developing his private library and plant collections (the world's finest), organizing expeditions, and acting as government advisor on the settlement of Australia (for which he earned the nickname "Father of Australia").

Many of the illustrations of the Australian plants were drawn or started by Sydney Parkinson, a wool dealer by trade who was so talented an artist that Banks took him under his wing. After his death during the return voyage, his drawings were completed by others and copper engravings were made. The British Museum, where the drawings had been available for consultation, finally had lithographs made from the engravings and published the collection in three parts between 1900 and 1905.

The first plate here shows the Australian violet, which usually has blue flowers. Occasionally, white-flowered forms are found. The second illustration shows a plant now called *Calandrinia*, a delicate pink-flowered member of the Portulaca family. *Byblis*, the third plant reprinted from this work, is a small insectivorous plant with blue flowers. All three illustrations would be suitable for use in delicate embroidery. Violets are always popular motifs for delicate handwork, but this one could become a bold design; try enlarging it for a striking needlepoint pillow or picture. The *Calandrinia* could be repeated several times to cover the entire surface of a pillow or other piece. The *Byblis* also lends itself to fine embroidery; it was used as a design for one of the Christmas tree ornaments shown on page 22.

Viola hederacea

Calandrinia quadrivalvis

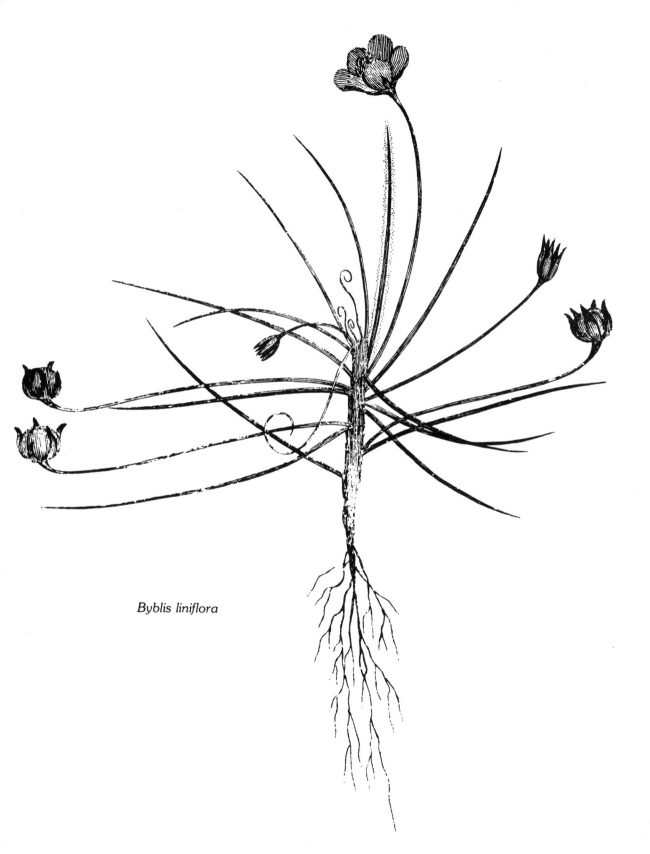

Byblis liniflora

47

1787
Botanical Magazine

Begun in 1787 by William Curtis, the *Botanical Magazine* is still published today, under the name *Curtis's Botanical Magazine*. The first issue consisted of three hand-colored copper engravings and a descriptive text. It sold for one shilling. The magazine appeared regularly on the first of the month throughout Curtis's lifetime and has continued in very much the same form to the present day, although the last hand-colored plate appeared in 1948.

A Quaker, Curtis was born in Hampshire, England, in 1746 and ran an apothecary business for several years before selling out to his partner in order to be free to pursue his botanical studies. He published several books, translated and illustrated some of Linneaus's work, held an appointment with the Society of Apothecaries of Chelsea, gave public lectures, and founded his own botanical gardens.

Although Curtis was an accomplished artist, authorities do not believe that he drew any of the illustrations that appeared in his magazine. Most of the plates published prior to 1815 were drawn by Sydenham Edwards, a Welshman whose art training was provided by Curtis. A skillful artist, Edwards also did the engraving for his early plates. They were hand-colored by William Graves, who carefully retained the spirit of Edwards's drawing. Curtis himself chose the plants to be illustrated; he sought the new and unusual for his audience, which had great enthusiasm for uncommon plants. The opening of China and Japan and the expanding Empire provided almost unlimited sources of new plants and throughout the great era of plant introduction exciting new species were first shown to the public by the *Botanical Magazine*. Noted botanists edited and wrote the text accompanying the illustrations, making the magazine an accurate record of the great age of plant hunting.

The five plates reproduced here are all from volumes one and two. The plants should be familiar to most of us today, although they were at one time oddities to European eyes. The first one, the small *Iris persica*, is related to the common, tall, garden Iris. Its fragrant white flowers are marked with blue. The second plate, the bold Nasturtium *Tropaeolum majus*, is a welcome summer flower in bright shades of red, orange, and yellow. The third illustration depicts the Cyclamen, which is often sold in the United States as a potted gift plant around Christmas time. Sporting brilliant pink, red, or white flowers which stand above the leaves, it is one of the most striking flowering plants you can have in your home. The last two illustrations show spring bulbs for the garden: the Crocus which has cheery flowers in white or shades of yellow or purple, and the Snowflake *Leucojum vernum*, a delicate flower whose white petals are tipped with green. The *Leucojum* flower was used for one of the Christmas tree ornaments shown on page 22.

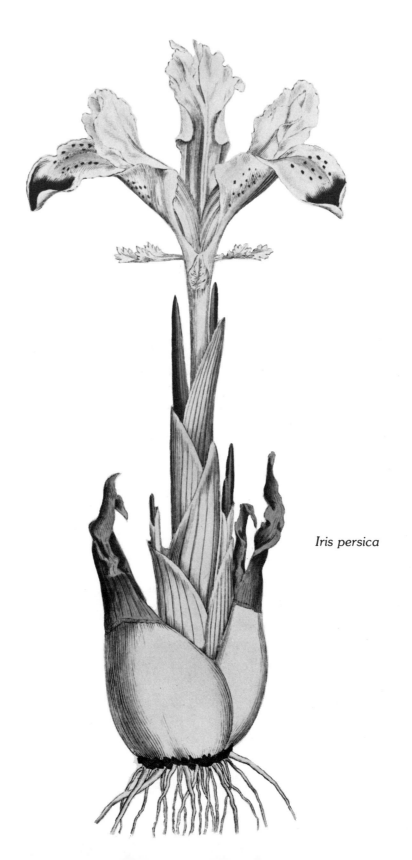

Iris persica

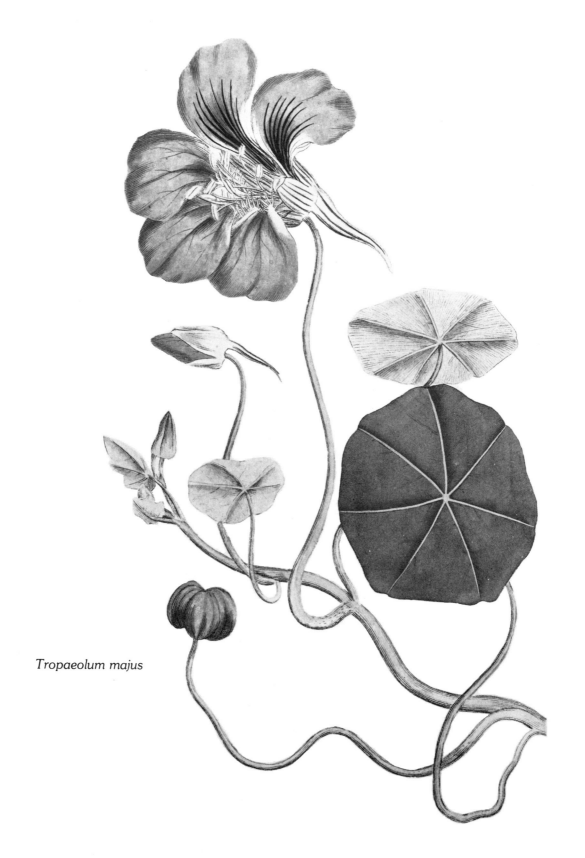

Tropaeolum majus

Cyclamen persicum

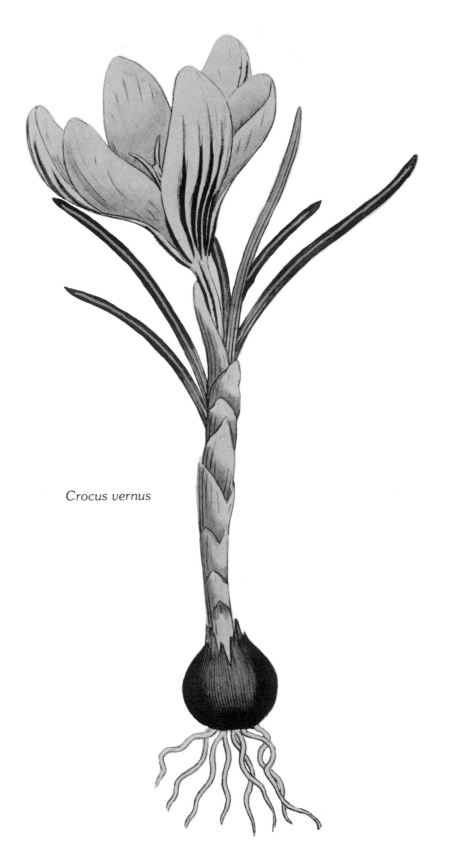

Crocus vernus

Leucojum vernum

1788
An History of
Fungusses

Present day botanical artists have at their disposal microscopes and other sophisticated equipment that enable them to see and accurately depict their subjects. Because the artists whose work is represented in this book had few such mechanical aids, the lower plants were poorly known and seldom depicted. The author of the earliest British works on fungi and ferns, James Bolton, had only "a little spy glass" to aid him, but his drawings were clear and accurate, as were the descriptions accompanying them.

James Bolton was a weaver and tavern keeper from Yorkshire, England, who sold illustrations of botanical, entomological, and ornithological subjects as well. His birthdate is unknown but he was an active and respected amateur naturalist from about 1750 until his death in 1799.

Bolton's second book, *An History of Fungusses Growing about Halifax*, was issued in parts between 1788 and 1791. He executed the 182 plates from his own water colors. For many years it was thought that his drawings for *An History of Fungusses* had been destroyed, but in the early 1930s they appeared in an antiquarian bookshop in Zurich and were purchased by the United States Department of Agriculture, in whose library they are now kept.

The four mushrooms reprinted from Bolton's book have interesting, almost abstract, shapes that lend themselves well to designing. Try embroidering an assortment of them in different sizes and in natural tones on a linen background for an unusual pillow or wall hanging.

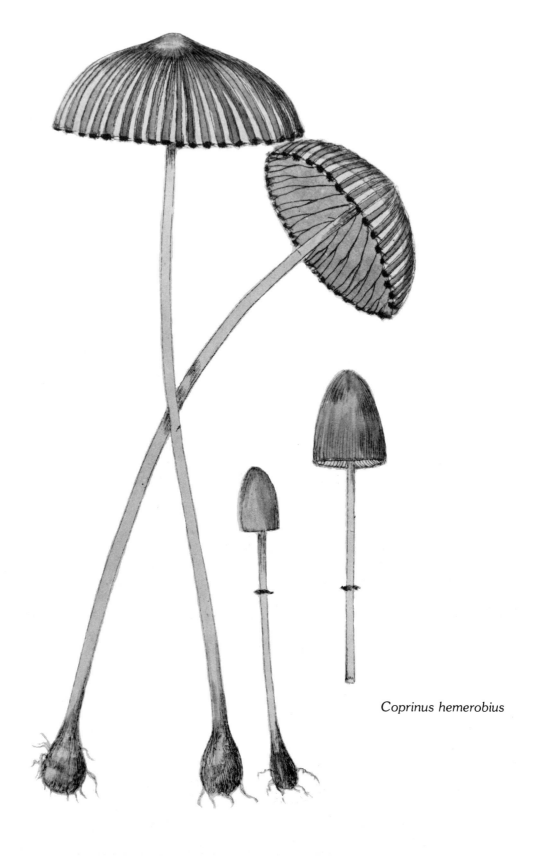

Coprinus hemerobius

56

Marasmius androsaceus

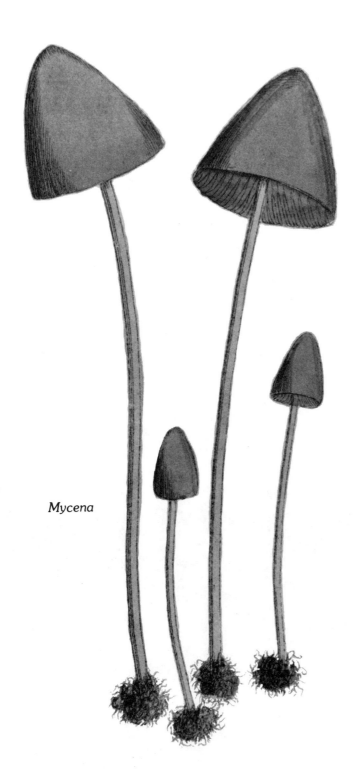

Mycena

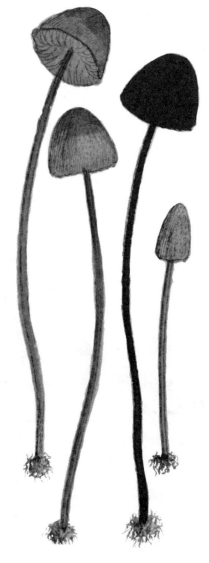

Panaeolus fimicola

1790
Filices
Britannicae

Ferns were the subject matter of the first book written by James Bolton, the English amateur naturalist who also produced *An History of Fungusses* from which the preceding plates were reprinted. This work, *Filices Britannicae*, was prepared during the 1780s and is sometimes considered to have been published in 1785, the date of the Introduction to Part One. The second part bears a publication date of 1790.

Although Bolton had never attempted etching before working on *Filices Britannicae*, he made his own plates for the book, following the careful drawings that resulted from his close observation of these lower plants. Many of these original drawings are held by the British Museum.

Like the mushrooms in his second book the four ferns depicted here make good design subjects. Any one of them could be used to decorate and make special something quite ordinary, such as a place mat, with part of the leaves repeated around the edge for a border.

Ophioglossum vulgatum

60

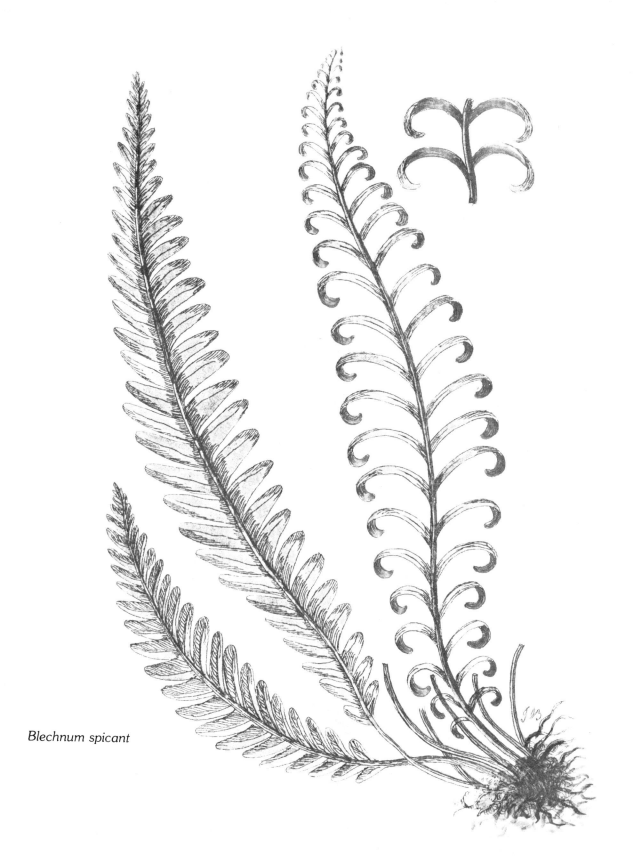

Blechnum spicant

Asplenium septentrionale

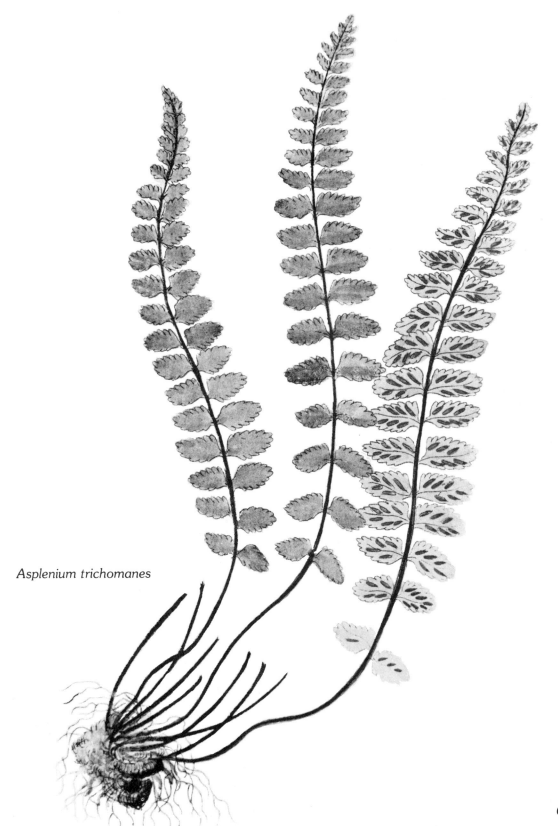

Asplenium trichomanes

63

1794
Oxalis

The second half of the eighteenth century was for Austria a high point in botanical studies, and the botanist who led this flourishing era was Nikolaus Joseph Jacquin. Born in Leiden, Holland, in 1727 to a family of French descent, he settled in Austria after studying philosophy, medicine, and botany at Louvain, Paris, and Vienna. In each of these cities he worked with well-known botanists and studied at university botanical gardens. His interest in plants soon overshadowed all else.

In 1755 Jacquin was chosen by Austria's Franz I to serve as the botanist on an expedition to the West Indies and South America to collect plants for the botanical garden at Schonbrunn, the royal palace in Vienna. After four years the expedition returned to Vienna with a large collection of living plants. Jacquin quickly published two books that are still important sources of information on West Indian flora and then went on to write numerous others describing the floras of various parts of the world according to the Linnaean system of classification. (Although Linnaeus and Jacquin never met, they corresponded and Jacquin became a staunch supporter of the Linnaean system.) Jacquin was a practical botanist whose energies were directed toward collecting and describing new plant species and as such he was remarkably successful. He held posts as professor of chemistry and botany and was Director of the University of Vienna botanical garden.

Jacquin's many books contained superb illustrations drawn either by Jacquin himself or by the best botanical artists of his time. Most were reproduced as copper engravings and were delicately hand colored. The illustrations reproduced here are from one of Jacquin's lesser-known works, *Oxalis*, devoted entirely to the genus *Oxalis*. Gardeners will recognize these plants because several species are grown in North American gardens or as house plants. The illustrations for this book were drawn by Johann Scharf, a talented artist who died of tuberculosis at the age of twenty-nine in the same year that the book was published.

Although similar, the four plants shown here have different forms and colors. The second and third are now considered to be the same species and may have red, pink, or white flowers. In Jacquin's book the drawings are colored as follows: the first has pale lavender flowers with yellow centers; the second has red flowers also with yellow centers; the third one has pure white flowers and leaves whose pale, lower surfaces contrast with their dark upper surfaces; and the last one has pink flowers and red-backed leaves.

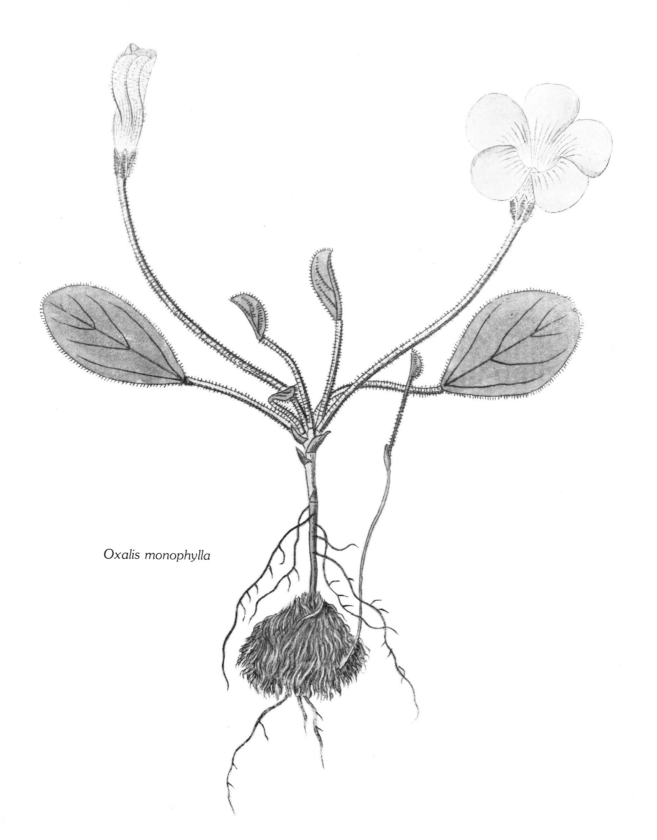

Oxalis monophylla

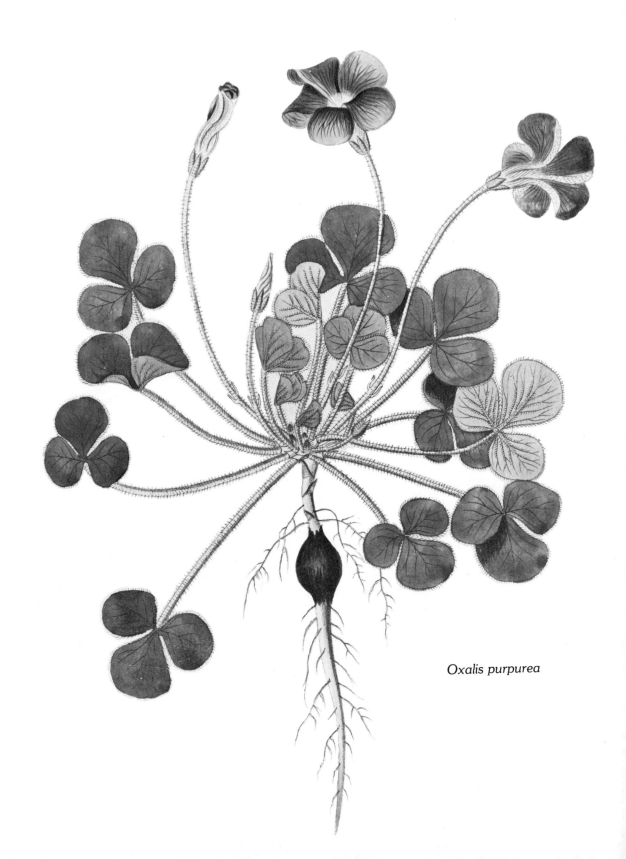

Oxalis purpurea

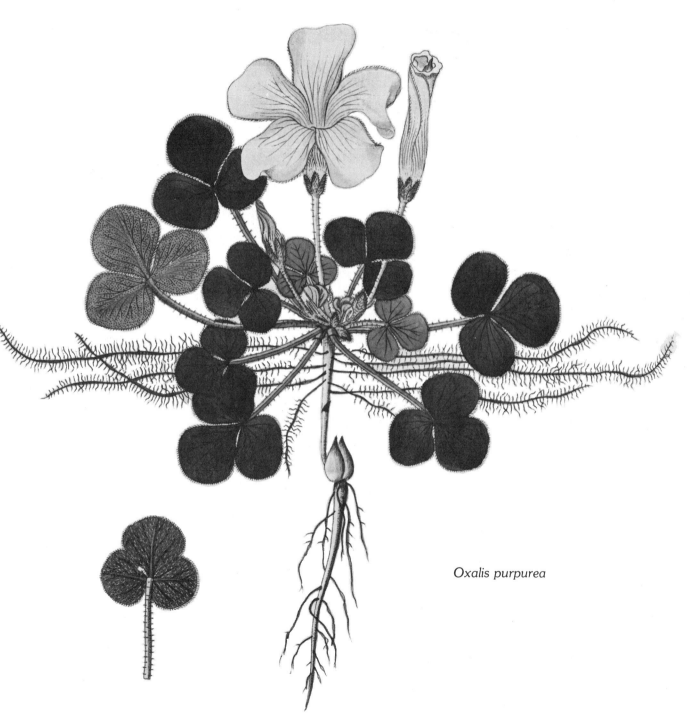

Oxalis purpurea

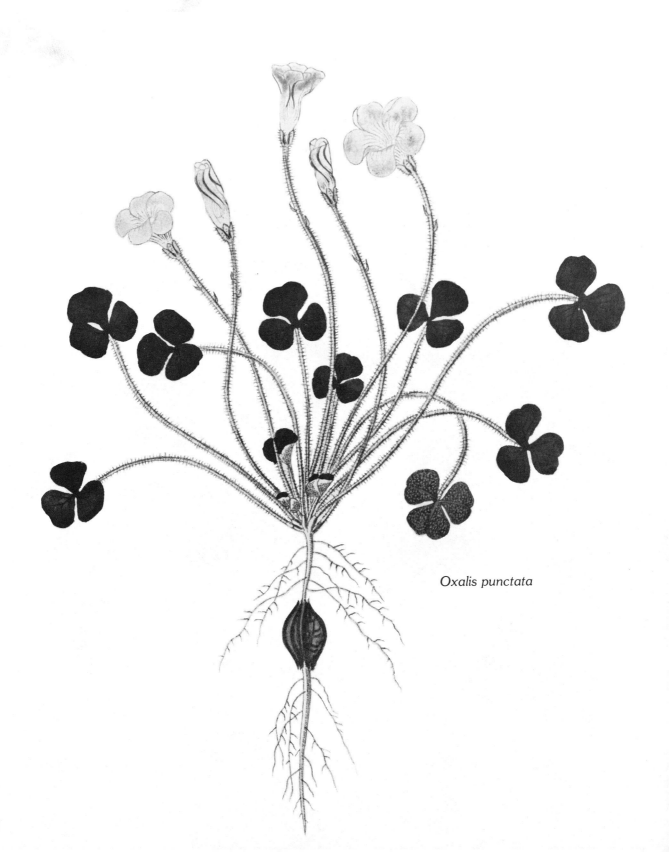

Oxalis punctata

1804
Novae Hollandiae Plantarum Specimen

The Australasian area attracted explorers, adventurers, and naturalists from many countries after Joseph Banks's tour during the years 1768-1771. The first decades of the eighteenth century marked the height of The Golden Age of Plant Exploration; it was a time during which new plants were being introduced to European countries at a dizzying pace (nearly 9,000 new plants were brought into England during the reign of King George III alone). Botanists and gardeners alike were always eager for more and the pace did not slacken during the nineteenth century.

France was among the countries that sent outstanding botanists on voyages of exploration and study of the South Pacific. One of them was Jacques Julien Houton de Labillardière, a prominent botanist whose contribution to the knowledge of Australasian plants was much greater than might be expected considering the fact that he made only one visit to that part of the world.

Labillardière served as naturalist aboard the vessel *Recherche* which, accompanied by the *Esperance*, sailed the South Seas from 1791-1794 collecting scientific data. The results of Labillardière's studies were published in his *Novae Hollandiae Plantarum Specimen*, which was issued in parts from 1804 to 1806, and in another work, *Sertum Austro-Caledonicum*, which was published twenty years later. (At that time Australia was called New Holland, having been so named by Dutch explorers.) These pioneering studies of Australian plants are important sources of information for researchers even today. There is a long list of Australian plants named after Labillardière, evidence of the importance of his botanical discoveries.

The gracefully drawn plants shown here were executed by Pierre Antoine Poiteau, who like Claude Aubriet and many other artists whose work is shown in this book, was a natural genius and self-made man. Born in 1766 the son of a poor thresher, his career began at the age of fourteen when he became apprentice gardener at a convent. He worked at several other gardens before being appointed to a position at the Jardin des Plantes in Paris, where he taught himself Latin, botany, and drawing and soon was assisting one of the professors who taught at the garden.

The French Revolution cost Poiteau his job, but an influential botanist arranged for him to join an expedition to Santo Domingo. Once there he had neither position nor income, but he nevertheless began collecting, studying, and drawing plants and was able to earn some money as a gardener. While in the New World, Poiteau met the young botanist Pierre Turpin, also a talented artist from a poor family. The two men became lifelong friends and collaborated on several major botanical publications, including the revision of Duhamel's *Traité des arbres fruitiers*.

After visiting the United States, Poiteau returned to France in 1801 with a large collection of plants. In the next few years he completed many of the illustrations for Labillardière's book. In 1815 he became head nurseryman at Versailles where he worked on the illustrations for Risso's *Histoire naturelle des orangers*. Later he was appointed Botanist to the King and Professor of Horticulture at the College de Fromont.

Throughout his life Poiteau devoted himself almost completely to the study of plants, receiving few rewards. It was not until the last years of his life that he began to receive the recognition he deserved and not until after his death that his talents were fully appreciated.

The seven plants illustrated here could be embroidered using very simple stitches, perhaps no more than the stem stitch, back stitch, and straight stitch. Small motifs such as the violet, a stem of *Billardiera,* the blue flower of the *Patersonia*, or a few stems of one of the grasses, could be adapted to decorate a child's dress.

Grasses are plants we often call weeds, but here they are delicate and beautiful. *Billardiera* is one of the many plants named for Labillardiere. It is shown in fruit; the berries are blue or violet colored. The violet is the same one illustrated in Banks's *Illustrations of Australian Plants*, but the treatment here is quite different. *Eryngium* is a small thistle-like plant with a bluish tint to it that grows along the seashore. The flowers are blue. The willowy, frail-looking *Hypoxis* is called the Golden Weather-glass because its yellow flowers close on cloudy days.

Patersonia glauca

71

Schoenus lanatus

Agropyron pectinatum

73

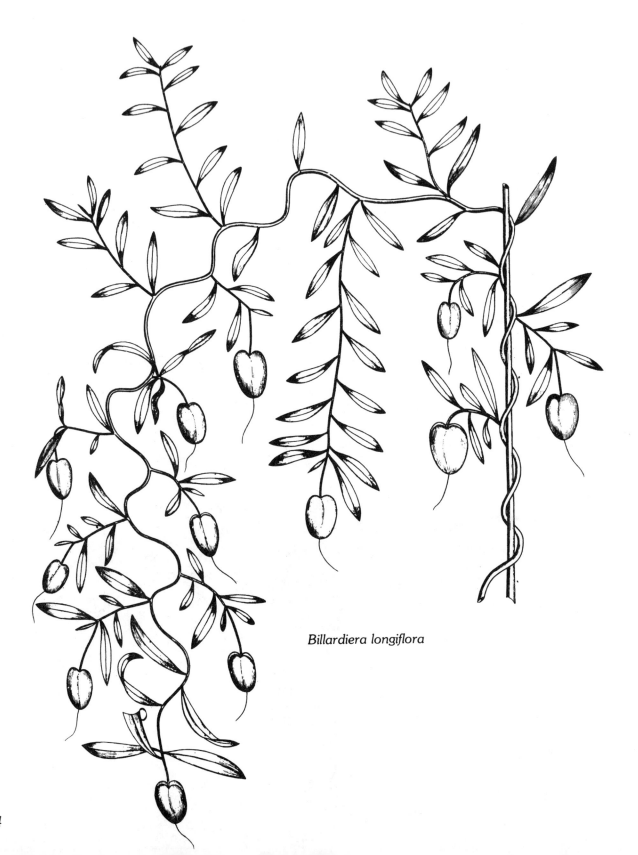

Billardiera longiflora

74

Viola hederacea

Eryngium vesiculosum

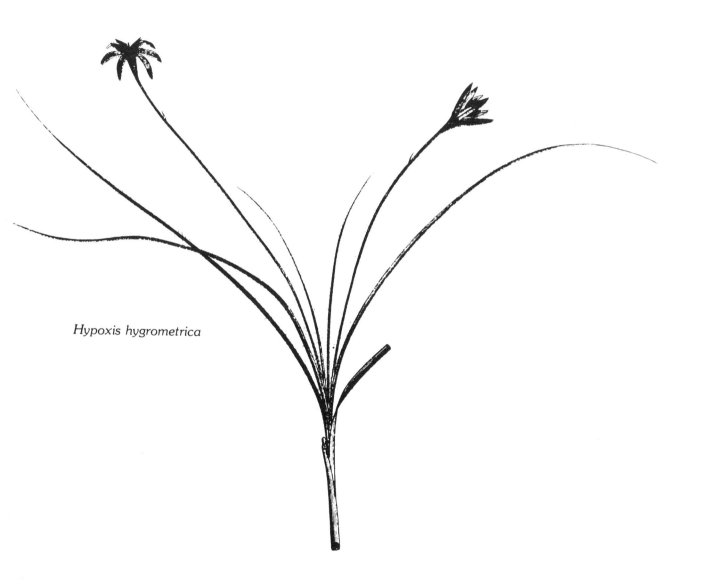

Hypoxis hygrometrica

1818
Histoire Naturelle des Orangers

The *Histoire naturelle des orangers* is a good example of those sumptuous books, carefully and expensively produced, that seem to contain so much of what was known about the natural world in eighteenth and nineteenth century Europe. Even more remarkable than the beauty of this book is the fact that it and all the other books discussed here were intended to be used, not simply admired. Pierre Antoine Poiteau's 109 delicately colored engravings were designed to help the reader identify the various types of citrus fruits. They can be appreciated equally well as works of art.

The text for this book was written by Antoine Risso, professor of physical and natural sciences at Nice, where he was born in 1777. He wrote numerous books on native and cultivated plants as well as on other branches of the natural sciences, but this work is his outstanding achievement.

The delicate designs within the fruit depicted in the three plates reprinted here could be adapted to many types of needlework and might even make you take a closer look at your morning orange or grapefruit. In cross section, they present beautiful examples of nature's symmetry. The cross section presents a simple design that could be repeated in several sizes and "citrus" colors to produce a striking abstract design. The complete drawings could be used to produce one or a set of embroidered pictures.

Citrus sinensis

79

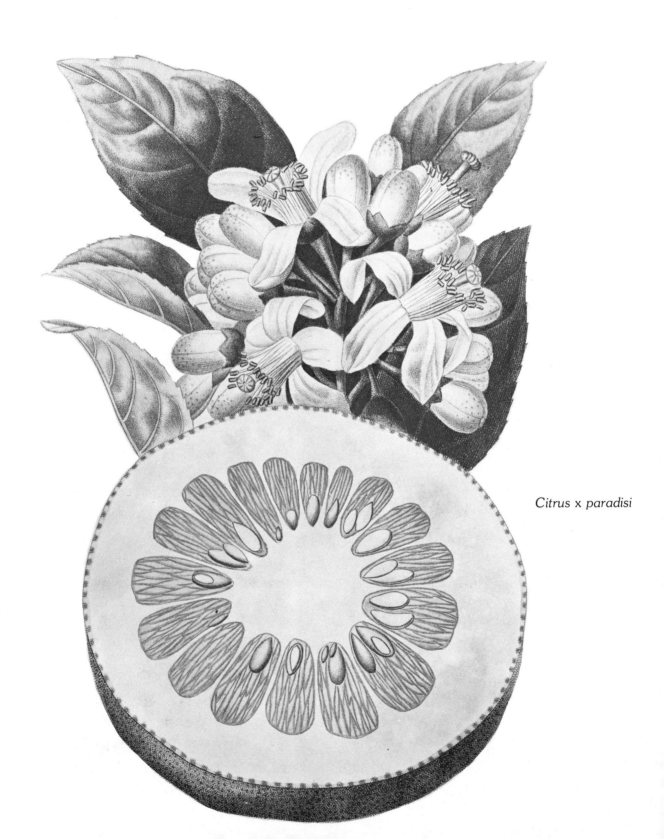

Citrus x *paradisi*

Citrus limon

81

1823
Recueil de Planches de Botanique

Jean Baptiste Lamarck's thinking reflected the changes brought about by the Enlightenment, the same questioning, antiauthoritarian attitudes that produced the French and American revolutions. Early in his life he believed that all forms of life exist now just as they were created. Later he believed in a more dynamic view of creation, one which permitted the development and diversification of plants and animals. Further expansion of such points of view by others and independent of Lamarck eventually led to the kinds of ideas expressed by Charles Darwin in his *Origin of Species*, published in 1859.

Lamarck was born in 1744, the eleventh child of an old Flemish family in Picardy, France. Lamarck had been singled out for the priesthood, but when he was barely seventeen, he ran away and joined the army. Within a few years poor health forced him to leave the military, and he began to study medicine, working in a bank to support himself. Before long his interest in botany overwhelmed all his other interests, and he devoted most of his energies to it. In 1778 he published his *Flore française* and four years later, as Botanist to the King, he began his *Dictionnaire de botanique*. Later Lamarck contributed to an encyclopedia called *Encyclopédie méthodique* which was planned as a successor to Diderot's famous *Grand encyclopédie*. The main text was called *Encyclopédie méthodique: botanique*.

Lamarck's contributions to the encyclopedia began to appear in 1791 and continued until 1817. Accompanying the main text was a synoptic review of the plant kingdom called the *Tableau encyclopédique et méthodique des trois regnes de la nature: botanique*. This synopsis was in turn accompanied by four volumes of illustrations published in 1823 and called *Recueil de planches de botanique de l'encyclopédie*. Plants from three of the plates that appear in the collection are pictured here.

These plates show three flowers that are grown in gardens today. Two species of *Bellium* are cultivated and may have white, yellow, or pinkish flowers. Gazania, the second plate reprinted here, seems to embody summertime and sunshine. Against the gray-green foliage, the flower heads look like suns themselves: brilliant orange, red, yellow, and even pink. One head may show several colors with flowers bearing either horizontal or longitudinal stripes. Take a look at a seed catalog to get an idea of the colors in these flowers if you're not familiar with them. The third plant shown is the familiar sunflower.

All three of these flowers are in the same botanical family and the similarity of their flowers is apparent. Combine them or use them separately in designs. Use them as outlines for a simple embroidered design or do the sunflower in crewel in several sizes on a pillow. A field of Gazanias would be particularly striking done as a traditional style hooked rug.

Bellium bellidioides

Gazania

Helianthus annuus

1826
Voyage Autour du Monde

Between 1817 and 1820, some years after Labillardière's visit, another French expedition explored the South Seas on the two ships *Uranie* and *Physicienne.* On board the *Uranie* was Charles Gaudichaud-Beaupré, the first French botanist to explore the Blue Mountains and Bathurst area in southeastern Australia. These expeditions were only two of many made by the French, who were very active in exploring this part of the world.

Because Gaudichaud was the first to visit this area, he collected many new plants, and, like Labillardière, his name is found in the names of many plants from Australia and other South Pacific islands. His *Voyage autour du monde,* from which the following illustrations were taken, was published in 1826. One hundred and twenty plates illustrate in clear detail some of the plants collected during this voyage. The plates were executed by the firm of A. Poiret. Gaudichaud returned to the South Seas on another ship, the *Bonité,* during the years 1836-1837, but by this time his health was declining so that the resulting publication, though containing many fine plates, was marred by the lack of factual information. Descriptive and explanatory material for this later book was never published so the book illustrated here remains Gaudichaud's *magnum opus.* He died in 1854 at the age of fifty-five.

These four simple, clear, outline drawings present interesting designs. The first two show leaves of ferns. The third, *Pratia,* is a small rock garden plant discovered by Gaudichaud in the Falkland Islands. It has pale rose violet flowers. The fourth, *Cymbonotus,* is an Australian plant with yellow flowers. Adopt them whole or in part as embroidery designs or use the ferns as abstract motifs for almost any type of needlework.

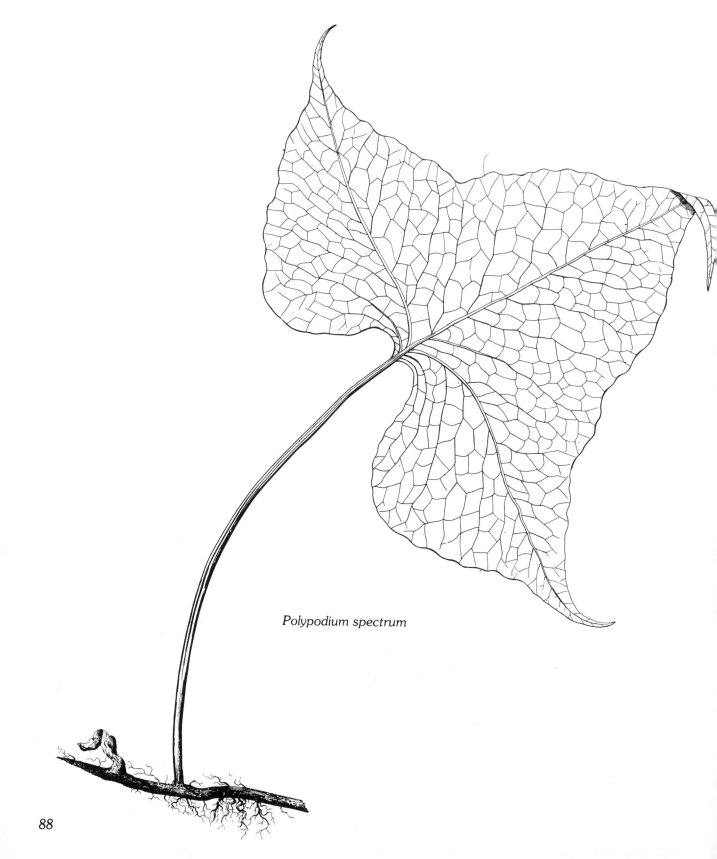

Polypodium spectrum

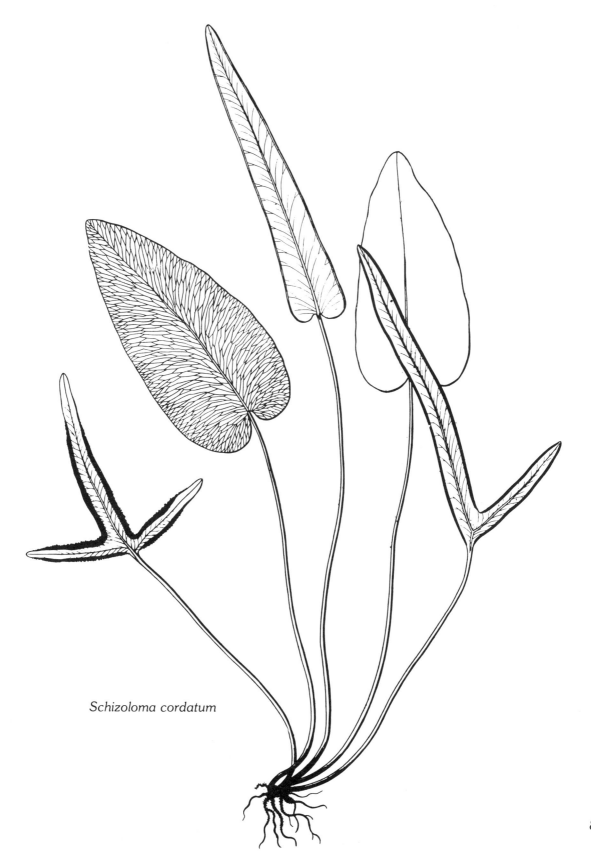

Schizoloma cordatum

89

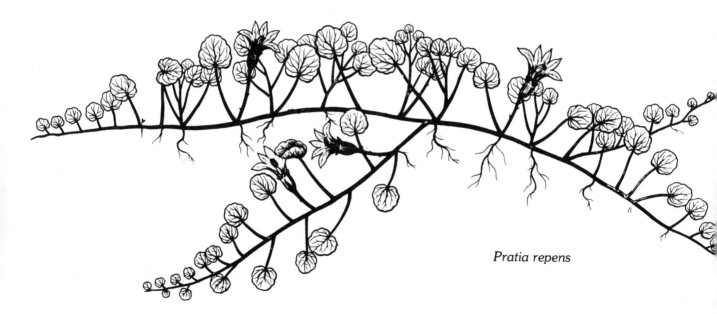

Pratia repens

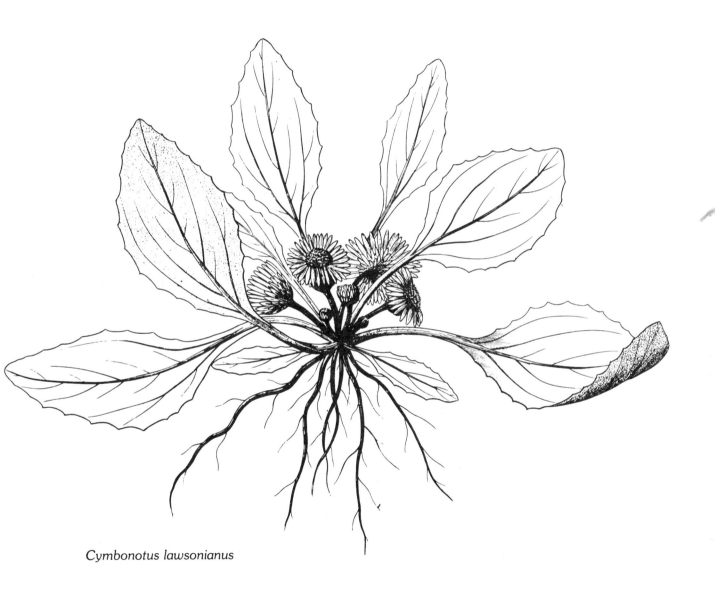

Cymbonotus lawsonianus

1836
Histoire Naturelle, Agricole et Économique du Maïs

Plants that have been domesticated and are grown for food often have fascinating histories, although many of them have been associated with man for so long that their true origins remain shrouded in mystery. One such plant is *Zea mays*, known in North America as corn and in Europe as maize. The story of corn has only recently begun to become clear, but it has intrigued agriculturists, writers, and artists for many centuries. One person to whom corn was especially important was Matthieu Bonafous, the agriculturist and humanitarian who wrote the remarkable book from which the following illustrations were taken.

Bonafous was born in 1794. Although French, his family had lived in northern Italy, and Bonafous claimed both countries as home. He was highly educated and during his lifetime pursued several careers and wrote many books, the first when he was barely twenty years old. His most consuming interests were agriculture and the improvement of rural living conditions. In fact, "Improve" might have been his motto.

In an effort to increase both the quantity and quality of agricultural products, he brought superior strains of domestic plants and animals into Europe. In 1841 he established an experimental garden in France where medicinal plants were introduced, grown, and distributed free of charge to the inhabitants of the Alpine valleys.

Bonafous felt corn had tremendous potential for improving the quality of life for the European peasant because he recognized its value as a food for both humans and animals. And to corn he devoted his largest and most lavish book. A New World plant, corn was not widely grown in Europe at the time of its publication, and Bonafous's *Histoire naturelle, agricole et économique du maïs* was the first comprehensive study that had been done. The book's pages covered all aspects of corn as understood at the time: its origins, varieties, culture, susceptibility to disease and insects, and its uses and value as an agricultural crop.

Bonafous believed that corn had been known in ancient China and other oriental countries during very early times and that it might have been transported to Europe by Arabs or Crusaders. Thus, crosses with later introductions from the Western Hemisphere would have produced the varieties cultivated in eighteenth and nineteenth century Europe. This view is now generally not accepted, although it has been argued until quite recently. It is now widely agreed that corn originated in Central America and was introduced into Europe and the Orient after Columbus's discovery of America.

About its ancient status there is no disagreement. Archaeological excavations in Mexico have revealed tiny ears of corn dating from 4000 B.C. In fact it has been cultivated so long that wild corn does not exist.

Matthieu Bonafous did much for agriculture by promoting corn as a crop plant and he has given us motifs that are both ancient and modern in these engravings of corn, a timeless symbol of harvest and plenty. The first drawing appeared on the opening page for the book's first chapter; it was a facsimile of a drawing in a Chinese book. The last two drawings were done by Angela Bottione-Rossi, an artist with the Botanical Garden at Turin. The bunch of three ears would make a unique and welcoming small rug, done in traditional hooking with delicately dyed wool.

Zea mays

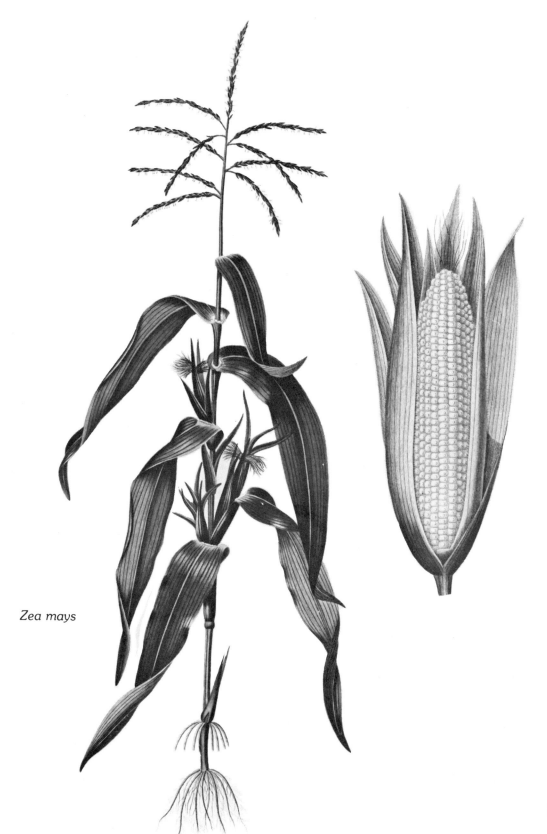

Zea mays

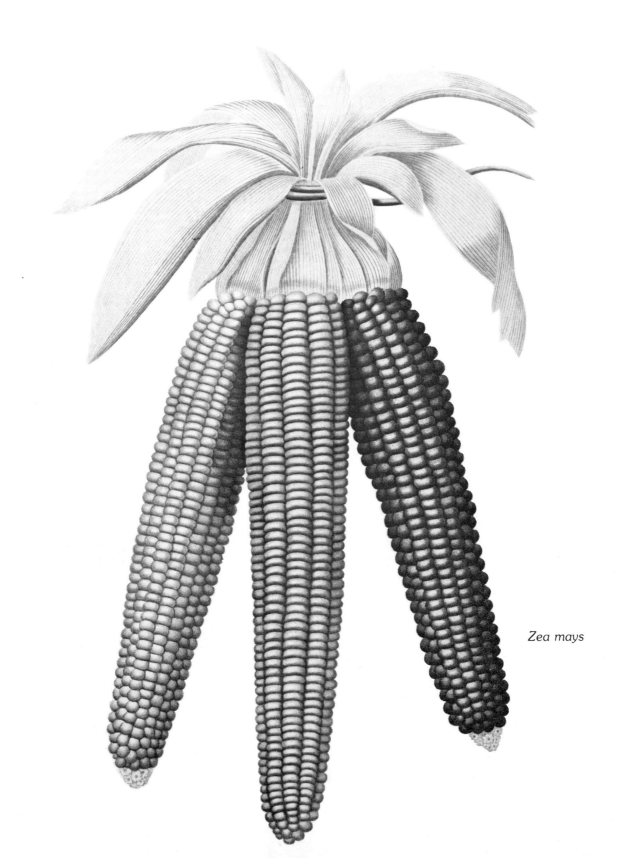

Zea mays

Appendix

Scientific Names of Plants Illustrated

The scientific names given here are those now assigned by botanists to the plants depicted in this book.

FLOWERING PLANTS

Sources of the Illustrations

Banks, Joseph. *Illustrations of Australian Plants Collected in 1770 During Captain Cook's Voyage Round the World in H.M.S. Endeavour.* Vol. 1. London: Trustees of the British Museum, 1900.

Bolton, James. *Filices Britannicae: An History of the British Proper Ferns.* Leeds: Printed for J. Binns, 1785-1790.

_____.*An History of Fungusses Growing about Halifax.* Huddersfield, Eng.: Printed for the author, 1788-1791.

Bonafous, Matthieu. *Histoire naturelle, agricole et économique du maïs.* Paris: Mme Huzard, 1836.

Botanical Magazine. Vols. 1 and 2. London. 1887-1889.

Colonna, Fabio. *Phytobasanos.* Naples: apud I.I. Carlinum & A. Pacem, 1592.

Duhamel du Monceau, Henri Louis. *Traité des arbres fruitiers.* Vol. 1. Paris: Saillant, 1768.

Gaudichaud-Beaupré, Charles. *Voyage autour du monde.* Paris: Pillet Ainé, 1826.

Jacquin, Nikolaus Joseph. *Oxalis.* Vienna: apud Christianum P. Wappler, 1794.

Labillardière, Jacques Julien Houton de. *Novae Hollandiae Plantarum Specimen.* Vol. 1. Paris: Mme Huzard, 1804.

Lamarck, Jean Baptiste. *Recueil de planches de botanique de l'encyclopédie.* Paris: Agasse, 1823.

Laurence, John. *The Clergyman's Recreation: Shewing the Pleasure and Profit of the Art of Gardening.* 5th ed. London: Printed for B. Lintott, 1717.

Risso, Antoine. *Histoire naturelle des orangers.* Paris: Imprimerie de Mme Herissant Le Doux, 1818-1822.

Rumpf, George Everard. *Herbarium Amboinense.* Vol. 5. Amsterdam: Apud Franciscum Changuion, J. Catuffe, H. Uytwerf, 1750.

van Reede tot Drakestein, Hendrick Adriaan. *Hortus Indicus Malabaricus.* Vol. 12. Amsterdam: Sumptibus viduae Joannis van Someren, haeredum Joannis van Dyck, Henrici & viduae Theodori Boom, 1703.

Some Basic Needlework Books

Coats and Clark, Inc. *One Hundred Embroidery Stitches.* Coats and Clark's Book No. 150. New York: Coats and Clark, 1964.

Collins, Carol Heubner. *Needlepoint: A Basic Manual.* Boston: Little, Brown & Co., 1976.

Enthoven, Jacqueline. *The Stitches of Creative Embroidery.* New York: Van Nostrand Reinhold Co., 1964.

Ireys, Katharine. *The Encyclopedia of Canvas Embroidery Stitch Patterns.* expanded ed. New York: Thomas Y. Crowell Co., 1977.

Monarch Press. *Monarch Illustrated Guide to Embroidery.* Introduction by Pam Dawson. New York: Monarch Press, 1977.

Parker, Xenia. *Hooked Rugs and Ryas: Designing Patterns and Applying Techniques.* Chicago: Henry Regnery Co., 1973.

Wilson, Erica. *Crewel Embroidery.* New York: Charles Scribner's Sons, 1962.

———.*Erica Wilson's Embroidery Book.* New York: Charles Scribner's Sons, 1973.